EVALUATION OF TRAINING

EVALUATION OF TRAINING

Martha Reeves

The Industrial Society

First published in 1993 by
The Industrial Society
Robert Hyde House
48 Bryanston Square
London W1H 2EA
Telephone: 0870 400 1000

Reprinted 1996, 1997, 1998, 1999, 2001

ISBN 1 85835 093 X
Ref 1621tw 6.01

British Library Cataloguing-in-Publication Data.
A catalogue record for this book is available from the
British Library

Typeset by: Photoprint, Torquay
Printed by: Optichrome, Woking
Cover design: Rhodes design

Text illustrations: Sophie Grillet
The Industrial Society is a Registered Charity No. 290003

Contents

Preface

The Importance of Training Evaluation

More and more companies and organisations are interested in finding out the impact of training on individuals within their organisations and on the bottom-line. Chairmen, managing directors, and heads of personnel departments are asking, "What did we get out of this training? Was it worthwhile in the end, considering the costs?" This book explains the purpose of evaluating training and gives an overview of the various methods used in the process.

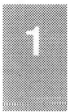

Training Evaluation and the Training Cycle

What is Evaluation?

Simply speaking, evaluation is the process of finding out how a course or any other training exercise has affected the organisation.

Evaluation versus Validation

Validation, a term often used synonymously with evaluation, refers to determining whether or not a course has met its prescribed objectives or whether or not a test or questionnaire is sound. It is a part of the evaluation process. For example, a trainer validates the content of a course by ensuring that it covers every objective it set out to cover or a questionnaire by making sure that it asks what is important to ask. This type of validity, referred to as content validity, is measured by making sure that the number of the items on a questionnaire, for example, corresponds appropriately with the amount of time spent teaching concepts and their importance. Roughly speaking, the more important the concepts and the more time spent on them during a course, the more test questions there should be covering these concepts; the less important the concepts and the less time spent on them, the fewer test questions there should be.

The word validation comes from the latin "validus" and the French "valere" meaning to be strong. In other words, in the training context a course is valid if its content is strong and appropriately reflects the course's objectives.

Evaluation, on the other hand, goes beyond the mechanics of course content, a test, or a questionnaire. Evaluation helps us measure many aspects of a training programme, from short term to long term effects.

The case of British Gas and Validation and Evaluation

British Gas uses a training design team to validate not only its courses but also tests. These tests are used during the training cycle to measure a trainee's mastery of course objectives. They are carefully designed and administered at various stages during the training process to check the standard of performance achieved. The team ensures that course content is relevant to individuals' jobs and that it reflects the course's objectives. British Gas evaluates its training by a very thorough process that includes:

- assessing the training as it is carried out so that problems can be dealt with as they arise.
- measuring the overall success of the training from the trainee's perspective.
- identifying areas of weakness in the training and making recommendations for change.
- determining whether trainees can transfer their learning from training to the job.
- looking at the costs versus the benefits of training from a financial perspective.
- analysing the perceived value of the training from all of those involved with it.

Evaluation and the Training Cycle

A traditional training model used several years ago addressed evaluation at the end of the training cycle, after implementation of the training. In this model, the trainer typically looked at the impact of the training after the training event and determined whether or not the training was a worthwhile exercise from the participants' point of view. Although this model addressed evaluation, it had its limitations. Because the trainer had not thought through the evaluation design before the training was designed, he or she was unable to compare the participants' pre-training learning or behaviours with their learning or behaviours after the exercise. Furthermore, the trainer could not set up control groups to compare with the trainee group unless he or she had thought of setting up the groups before the training event. The trainer was primarily limited to asking the participants for their reactions to the training.

A newer, more useful model recognises that the designer of

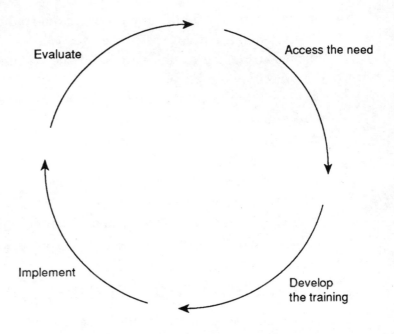

Fig. 1.1   The Old Training Cycle

the training needs to determine the evaluation design of the training soon after identifying the training need. Knowing the evaluation design upfront allows the evaluator to collect valuable baseline data about the participants and the organisation that might otherwise be difficult to collect after the training exercise. For example, the evaluator may decide to use pre and post test scores of the participants as part of the evaluation design. He or she would need to test the participants before the training exercise to obtain a comparison of each individual's knowledge before and after the training event and to make a judgment about how much the participants learned from the training event. In the new model, evaluation can occur anywhere along the process. For example, in addition to evaluating the long

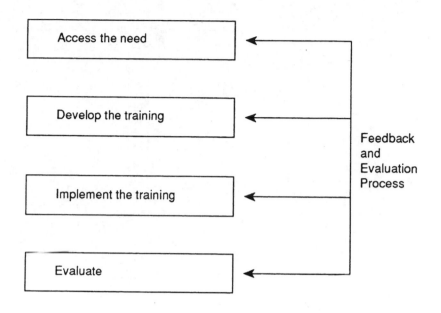

Fig. 1.2   The New Training Cycle

term effects of training on participants, the evaluator might decide to evaluate the course as it is taking place so that he or she can modify the content to make it even more effective.

Another view of the New Training Cycle is the 'endless belt' of training and development, which shows how *validation* is intrinsically linked to design and delivery and how *evaluation* is linked to objectives and outcomes. It also places the *results* in context of the organisation's needs.

British Gas' "Systems Approach To Training" exemplifies this newer approach to evaluation. In the training design phase, it determines evaluation methods that will be used

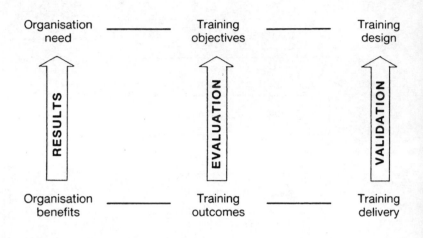

Fig. 1.3   The 'Endless Belt' of Training and Development

and allows for feedback about the training at several stages so that it can continuously improve training.

The Kirkpatrick Model

One of the most widely used models for classifying the levels of evaluation, used by Barclays Bank PLC and others, comes from Kirkpatrick. His model looks at four levels of evaluation, from the basic reaction of the participants to the training to its organisational impact. The intermediary levels examine what people learned from the training and whether or not the learning affected their behaviour on the job. Level one concerns itself with the most immediate reaction of participants and is easily measured by simple questionnaires after the training event. Level two, harder to measure than level one, is concerned with measuring what people understood and how they were able to demonstrate their learning. Level two might be measured by paper and pencil ability tests or job simulations. Level three looks at whether and how people's behaviour on the job, in terms of their job performance, changed. For example, after a writing skills course, did individuals make fewer grammatical and spelling errors and were their memos easier to understand? Level four, "result", is most difficult to measure. It focuses on the organisational, rather than individual, impact of the training. Did the training influence the bottom-line? Did it improve morale? For example, a training course on using a particular piece of equipment might have reduced downtime and therefore improved overall productivity. Another on developing a personal development plan might have had a positive impact on staff morale. Depending on the type of training and the availability of resources (time, money and staff), the evaluation may focus on all levels or look at only a few levels. Measuring the organisational impact may not be relevant for every type of training event.

The Kirkpatrick Model

Level 1 (Reaction)	How did the participants react to the programme?
Level 2 (Learning)	What did individuals learn?
Level 3 (Behaviour)	What are the long term effects of the training on individuals' job performance?
Level 4 (Result)	How did the company or organisation benefit from the exercise? What was the organisational impact?

The Ciro Framework of Evaluation

Another way of looking at evaluation is to ask three basic questions, "What needs to be changed?", "What is likely to bring about the desired changes?", "What suggests that a change has actually taken place?". This approach, developed by Warr, Bird, and Rackham, is called the Ciro Framework because the acronym refers to context, input, reaction, and outcome evaluation. Let's look at these four levels.

Context Evaluation

Context evaluation answers the question, "What needs to be changed?" Within context evaluation, the trainer looks at ultimate objectives, intermediate objectives and immediate objectives. For example, what defect in the organisation is the trainer ultimately hoping to change? What intermediary objectives, such as changes in employees' work habits, would the trainer like to influence? And finally, what immediate skill, knowledge or attitudes do employees need to acquire before the intermediary objectives can be met?

Input Evaluation

Input evaluation answers the second question, "What is likely to bring about the desired changes?" Here the trainer must evaluate his or her resources and decide on the best way to proceed. Questions about budget, staff, merits of different training techniques, external versus internal resources would be asked at this stage.

Reaction Evaluation

Obtaining participants' reactions to a course either during or after the event can be a useful part of the evaluation exercise. Uncovering reactions of participants could be done formally through questionnaires or informally over coffee breaks, in the hotel bar, or during conversations several weeks after the training. Lucas Areospace Ltd. found it useful to involve non-trainers in the reaction stage of the evaluation process. The training manager discovered that feedback was more honest when course evaluation forms were administered by a disinterested party.

Outcome Evaluation

Warr, Bird and Rackman have identified four stages of outcome evaluation: defining training objectives, selecting measurements for these objectives, measuring the objectives at the appropriate time, and assessing the results to improve the training. Defining training objectives would have been done as part of the context evaluation. The primary purpose of this stage of the evaluation process is for trainers to improve their product; the results of outcome evaluation allow trainers to go back and refine current training and plan future training. Three levels of outcome evaluation relate to the extent to which the individual is affected. Immediate outcomes refer to changes in the knowledge, skills or attitudes of individuals as measured immediately after the training. Intermediate outcomes look at how individuals have changed their on-the-job behaviour. Ultimate outcomes measure how a department or an entire organisation has changed.

One can see similarities between the Kirkpatrick model and the Ciro framework. The outcome evaluation part of the Ciro framework parallels the learning, and behaviour, and result parts of the Kirkpatrick model, for example. The

Ciro framework differs from the Kirkpatrick model in its trainer-centred approach. The input part of the model is clearly focused on what trainers have available to them in terms of resources.

Overall Purposes of Evaluation

No matter which model you choose to adopt, all have similar aims. Evaluation can help you understand the following:

- the strengths and weaknesses of a current training programme.
- the impact of training on individuals.
- the impact of training on the organisation.
- who should participate in further training programmes.
- who benefitted the most and least from the training exercise.
- the costs versus the benefits of training.
- specifically the areas individuals should continue to focus on for their own development.

Examples of uses of Evaluation in Organisations

Organisations in the U.K. use evaluation for a variety of purposes as shown above. Dow Chemicals have used evaluation for refining its quality course, designed to change Dow to a more customer-focused organisation. The course, covering W.E. Deming's basic quality tools, is evaluated by the regional quality manager, trainers and the regional training manager. Detailed course questionnaires were administered to participants before and after the training. The questionnaires revealed that course partici- pants did not understand all of the content proposed on the two day course. The Dow evaluation focused on the immediate learning of participants and the strengths and weaknesses of the training rather than application of skills or business impact.

Cussons UK undertook an evaluation of its total quality management training that revealed an impact on course participants and the organisation. The two day course and two day follow-up session for project leaders was designed to instill total quality tools and techniques and to ensure everyone understood the vision and values of Cussons. The total quality steering committee and quality director took ownership for the evaluation which used a variety of methods. Post-course evaluation forms, action plans, progress reports from project work, verbal updates during projects, and evaluation by team and project leaders were used. The central finding of the evaluation was that managers were using total quality techniques in their work and that projects were yielding savings to the company.

Glasgow City Council's training of first-line supervisors focused on the learning that was transferred to the job and highlighted future training efforts and to whom they should be directed. The course's objective was to encourage first line supervisors to take more control over their management responsibilities and to empower them to assume more authority. The evaluation consisted of post-course presentations, "action tasks" between the course modules that ensured that the participant had achieved the objectives of the module, a work-based project that identified the extent to which the participant had transferred the learning to his or her job. The evaluation uncovered cost savings and service improvements and targeted more supervisors for future training.

Evaluation – an art not a pure science

Although evaluators should attempt to validate their evaluation tools (questionnaires, tests etc.), much of evaluation is an art rather than a science. There are always choices of evaluation methods and subjectivity on the part of evaluators. When unstructured interviewing is used as an evaluation technique, interviewers interpret and analyse the interviews from their own perspectives. Measuring the costs versus the benefits of training involves a good bit of creativity; one evaluator may choose to include many intangible benefits while another may stick to only items that have a hard value in terms of currency.

Summary

- *Evaluation is the process of finding out how a course has affected participants and the organisation.*
- *Validation is interested in finding out whether a course truly reflects its objectives in terms of content and emphasis on specific content areas.*

- *The training cycle should consider evaluation at several stages not just at the end of the cycle.*
- *The Kirkpatrick model of evaluation looks at Reaction, Learning, Behaviour and Result.*
- *The Ciro Model of evaluation examines Context, Input, Reaction and Outcome.*

The Importance of Evaluation and a Company's Public Image

Several well recognised national contests or awards recognise the importance of training evaluation. Two notable awards include specific guidelines for the evaluation of training. They are The National Training Award and The Investors In People Award. These awards not only encourage effective evaluation but also go a long way to promote a positive company image to the public.

The Investors in People Award

The Investors in People Award uses four criteria for judging organisations: commitment, planning, action, and evaluation. It is awarded to organisations that make a public commitment from the top to develop all employees. Organisations must show a commitment to communicate a vision to all employees of where they are going and allow each employee to contribute to that vision. Training and development needs must be routinely assessed and linked to the business plan. Actions taken should meet the needs of all existing staff and new recruits and individuals should have input into their own job-related development needs. The Investors in People Award does not stipulate how an organisation should evaluate its training. Instead, it sets out the following guidelines for evaluation:

- The competence, commitment and the skills of employees should be reviewed at all levels against business goals and targets.
- The effectiveness of training and development needs to be reviewed at the top level and this must lead to renewed commitment.

Examples of Evaluation and the Investors in People Award

Several organisations have won the Investors in People Award; a few that have developed interesting evaluations of their training are mentioned here. Braintree District Council continually compares staff performance with its business plan. It looks to see if and to what extent its service targets have been met. Internal customer surveys help measure how well the council's employees are achieving back on the job. Dow Corning uses several approaches to evaluate its training including feedback from employees, measurement of safety standards and customer complaints, staff turnover rates, shipping performance, and more

qualitative measures such as employee morale and the feeling of a team spirit. Alternative Travel Group measures the success of its training for trip managers and leaders by constant evaluation of their progress. Customer surveys ask questions about the management and people skills of specific trip leaders and trip managers. Furthermore, each individual in the organisation works on a personal development plan that is tied to the evaluation results from the customer surveys as well as the individual's own aspirations. In assessing its training efforts, Lonrho Textiles, in

Northumberland, examined pre-training and post-training retention rates of employees under 25 years old. IDV UK, a drinks manufacturer and subsidiary of Grand Metropolitan, used credit control to evaluate its training. Faced with increased competition, it needed to train staff to better respond to customers and help collect invoices faster. The company's credit controllers were trained to act as financial advisors rather than debt collectors. In evaluating the training, it examined how long customers took to pay bills and improvements in cash flow. After the training, the time span for customer payment was reduced by 15%.

The National Training Award

The aim of the National Training Award is to identify organisations that excel in training and development and link their training and development programmes to business outcomes. Evaluation has a role to play in this link of the organisation's training to business performance. Judging panels consider what the training actually achieved, what measures were used to evaluate the training, and how the training met an organisational need. Effective training outcomes might be soft or hard; improvement in role perception or morale of trainees might be looked at along side harder measures such as percent increase production or reduced error rates.

Examples of National Training Award Winners

Eighty public and private organisations a year have been selected for the award since its inception in 1987. A few organsations, highlighted below and on pages 18 and 19, exemplify good evaluation practices. In 1986 and 1987,

Sainsbury's undertook a 12 day course in cooperation with the Department of Trade and Industry to train pre-recruits for its new inner city North Kensington store. It used a control and experiment group to evaluate the effectiveness of the training programme. Of the 49 participants who finished the course, 77% were offered employment by Sainsbury's, compared with 41% of individuals who applied without the training. The trainees also had a higher retention rate compared with the non-trainee group: 69% as opposed to 40%. The Metropolitan Police Force of Greater London found it needed to revamp its outmoded training to its officers. It evaluated its four training modules via peer assessment and line manager pre-training and post-training observations. Thomas Cook won the award for its training of branch managers to tap the small and middle size corporate market. The evaluation was conducted in stages over a nine month period. The goal of the programme was for each branch manager to gain new business worth at least 50,000 and boost business from existing clients by at least 5% within a twelve month period. These goals were reached within three months instead of the twelve month objective. Rank Xerox had a particular challenge when it relocated its electronic manufacturing plant. Because many of its workforce were not prepared to move, it was faced with hiring and training new workers. Training programmes were developed for each job function and a 24 hour Open Learning Centre was established. The success of the training and Open Learning Centre were measured by a comparison of the old plant site with the new plant site. Daily worker outputs increased by an average of 9%, production per person per day went up by 35%, and errors were reduced by 17%. Allen and Hanburys, a subsidiary of Glaxo, used sales targets and client surveys to measure the effectiveness of its training to its salespeople on Serevent, a new asthma medication. After the training, the sales force met its six month target in half the time and surveys indicated that six months after the product launch 98% of general practitioners were aware of Serevent and 65% of them had prescribed it.

BS 5750

The British Standards 5750 is a quality assurance standard given to those British companies that have been recognised by independent assessors to have attained a degree of quality directly related to their customer's requirements. Although the standard does not specify how a company should evaluate its training, two clauses in the BS 5750 literature suggest the importance of training and training evaluation. The first says that the supplier shall identify training needs and provide necessary training among all personnel who affect quality during production and installation of the product. The second clause discusses the importance of internal quality audits to ensure the effectiveness of the quality system. As training is an important part of any quality programme, these audits would naturally be used as one form of evaluation of training.

Summary

- *Training awards enhance the public image of an organisation.*
- *Both The Investors In People and the National Training Award stress the importance of evaluation and judge entrants based on how well they evaluate the impact of training.*
- *The BS5750, a quality standard, stresses measurement of all quality efforts and all processes affecting the customer.*

The Who, What, When and Where of Evaluation

Who Should Be Involved?

As you are putting together the evaluation design, think about who should be involved and in what capacity. Advantages to using other individuals include the following: they will be more involved and will, therefore, better understand the nature of the training process; because of their association with the training department, they will bring it more visibility; the evaluation process will be viewed as less biased and not exclusively the perceptions of the training department who may be seen to have a vested interest in the outcome; and finally, using others will help you stretch your human resource.

The Role of the Senior Manager

Senior managers may be involved in evaluation as evalu-ators or in helping to map out the evaluation design. If senior managers review the evaluation when it is completed, it is useful to obtain their support at the early stages. If they understand and have had a voice in the methods you plan to use, explaining the results of the evaluation at the end of the process will be far easier. Generally speaking, the more important the training exercise the more critical it is to involve senior level managers. When organisations are in a period of planned change or a period of instability or turbulence, the visibility of the senior management group in any training effort is critical.

At American Express, senior level managers are helping to evaluate a worldwide leadership training course by providing short case study examples of how they have seen leadership principles applied in the workplace and by documenting any changes they have noticed in employee behaviour. These testimonials by the senior management group are included with other perspectives such as the opinions of the participants themselves and the opinions of the participants' direct reports via an "Upward Feedback" tool.

The Use of External Evaluators

External evaluators may be useful in some situations. The evaluation project, if large, may require an effort greater than the resources available internally. An external evaluator may provide the expertise and experience that no one internally has. Moreover, because they do not personally know the trainees or others involved in the evaluation, they will be more objective. ICL used outside consultants to help evaluate its "core technical programme" and to help set down a systematic process for all of its future evaluations. Using questionnaires and interviews with participants over a period of time, the consultants found that the programme improved efficiency, increased the trainee's confidence, and better prepared the trainees for future roles in the company.

The Role of the Line Manager in Evaluation

The line manager may be particularly suited to help out with the evaluation when it concerns tracking the progress of his or her employees. He or she may help the evaluators consider what type of follow-up activities would be useful and which would be relatively easy to monitor. The first level manager may be the best individual to track behavioural or attitudinal changes in the trainee. Increased confidence or a positive work ethic, for example, is something on which a first level manager may be able to comment. Line managers may be able to collect samples of their trainees' work. For example; to evaluate the long term impact of a writing skills course, line managers in one organisation kept samples of their direct reports' memos and letters over a six month period, at one month intervals. The line managers looked for number of spelling errors, grammatical errors, awkward sentence structure and punctuation errors. They also wrote a brief summary about how their direct reports improved. These writing samples and summaries were then turned into an evaluation chairman who analysed the information. In another situation, line managers were well suited to observe their direct reports to see if and how they had changed their attitudes about

working in a team. In partnership, line managers and trainers evaluated a team building course. In a journal, line managers documented examples where their employees used teamwork effectively and wrote verbatim comments made by their direct reports that suggested they were behaving as a team.

A Partnership of Line Manager and Trainer

The Royal National Theatre offers a good example of cooperation between line managers and the training department. Trainers and line managers meet to determine the training objectives and to specify measurable outcomes. The trainers conduct a training needs analysis to identify gaps in knowledge, skills, and attitudes and then design the training to fill these gaps. Trainers also design the evaluation methods to determine the success of individuals and groups. In addition, they design course validation methods to ensure that the training meets its objectives and provide information to enable course redesign as necessary. Line managers agree to design a methodology for evaluating the organisational benefits of the training. They specify the evaluation criteria and set the parameters for improvement at the organisational level.

The Role of the Second Level Manager

Second level managers may not be able to effectively observe day to day work habits of individuals who are one step removed from them. They may, however, be able to document changes in attitude or outward behaviour that seem to be having an affect on the business. The Director of a Client Service department, after a course on customer care, may find that she receives fewer complaint letters and fewer angry phone calls. She may also describe an atmosphere in the office where individuals seem to be handling customer calls beyond five p.m., the normal "quitting" time. This sort of testimonial evidence from someone deemed important in the organisation is a powerful part of the evaluation process.

The Role of the Course Participant

Self-evaluation is an integral part of most evaluations. Participants evaluate their reaction to the course via questionnaires distributed at the end of the course. They may also help evaluate their own learning after the course. For example, a group of trainees may fill in action plans describing how they are using the training or may describe how their attitudes have been affected as a result of the training. At one airline company, computers were installed at various locations in the organisation to help track how employees' attitudes might have changed as a result of several initiatives, including training. Employees simply worked at a computer station and answered a set of questions about how they felt about several issues. These attitude evaluations were tracked over time to see if the training had had a positive impact on employees' attitudes. The computer offered a non-threatening evaluation device for asking sensitive questions which might have been difficult for an evaluator to ask in person. At Phillips, training participants fill in a detailed action plan after the training event in which they document what they learned from the event, whether or not they achieved their personal objectives, their opinion about the content of the course and the methods used and their further training and development needs. At six months time, the participant, his or her line manager, and a personnel or training specialist revisit the participant's action plan to determine what has been done and to evaluate the course again from the perspective of having completed the training six months ago.

It is important to approach an evaluation project from more than one perspective. Self-evaluation can be biased. Individuals have a hard time coming to grips with their own shortcomings and may over-evaluate their progress. Furthermore, individuals may not trust the anonymity of the evaluation process. They may think that their results will be shared with others, in spite of the fact that they have been told otherwise. This distrust of how the findings may be used may cause some participants to respond dishonestly. To ensure your results are sound, evaluate from a variety of viewpoints: the line manager, the trainer, and the participant, for example. Look for the consistent themes among and between the various evaluators.

Although using other people is generally a good idea, it has its drawbacks. If you use line managers, you will need to allow additional time to train them in evaluation methods. What you can gain on establishing the process as a more objective exercise, you may lose on the inconsistency of approach. For example, in spite of your efforts to train line managers, some will be less effective evaluators than others. Some may do a very thorough job, while others may give only cursory evaluations. The best way to limit this inconsistency is to provide specific instructions for evaluators, thoroughly brief them, and allow them to practice the evaluation technique you are using. For example, if observations are part of the evaluation design, you would provide a standard explanation of what you'd like them to observe (this might be in the form of a checklist), explain how to conduct an observation and provide at least one practice session.

Setting up an Evaluation Committee

Consider setting up a cross functional evaluation committee through which you can gain acceptance for your evaluation design and any evaluation tools that you create. This committee can help you test out ideas before you implement them and may play the devil's advocate, helping you weigh the pros and cons of specific approaches. A word of caution. Select individuals for the committee carefully and keep the group small. Three or four people may be sufficient.

The chart on p. 28 highlights who might be involved in the evaluation process and the pros and cons involved in their participation.

What to Evaluate?

The question of what to evaluate is best answered by, "What do we want to find out and how feasible is it to find out?" Before the training is conducted or designed, look at the training objectives. The objectives should help you determine what you want to evaluate. Look, also, at the Kirkpatrick levels of evaluation. Are you interested in knowing only participants' reactions to the training? Are you interested in what people learned from the training and how this learning translated to on-the-job performance? Are you hoping to find out whether the training exercise influenced staff turnover or the bottom-line? Ask yourself whether or not you have enough data and whether or not it makes sense to try to establish these relationships. It may be foolhardy to suggest that a management training course caused company profits to soar, especially if other factors (deregulation, a plunge in the cost of raw materials, new leadership or better vendor relationships) more than likely caused the change. In a different scenario, you may be able to establish that intensive training on the effect of absentee-

	External Evaluators	Line Managers	Senior Managers	Human Resources or Training Dept.
PROS	– specific expertise and experience in evaluation methods. – objectivity	– increased commitment to the evaluation process. – increased visibility for the training evaluation.	– high visibility for the training evaluation project. – senior managers could help map out evaluation strategy and design.	– usually committed to the process. – could be more knowledgeable than other groups.
CONS	– costs	– time commitment necessary to train line managers. – varying degrees of ability (some evaluators will be better than others).	– may not realistically have the time to help.	– if no other evaluators are used, could be seen to be self-serving.

ism caused fewer absences, which in turn positively affected productivity.

When to Evaluate?

Evaluation can take place at various stages during the training process. Circulating feedback questionnaires to participants during a training exercise can give the trainer valuable information. He or she may decide to alter the content of the course or adjust the level of difficulty based on the feedback.

The evaluation team could examine the impact of the training during several timeframes. For example, the team may want to know the impact of a written communications training one month, six months and one year after the training to see of participants are applying the concepts on the job and to see if their direct reports, peers and superiors are benefitting as recipients of their communication. Written communication samples might be analysed from these timeframes and interviews with direct reports, peers, and superiors could be conducted to find out their opinions.

Where to Evaluate?

In deciding where to evaluate participants, you will need to think about the impact on the trainees and others. Evaluation procedures should be as unobtrusive to the flow of business as possible, but also obtain valuable information. You'll need to weigh the pros and cons of face to face contact with trainees via observation or interviews against questionnaires that can be completed anonymously and turned in by a deadline, for example. Part of the evaluation might be done at a distance via questionnaires, part of it may be done via on-the-job observations, and some may be done via focus groups, bringing small groups of individuals together in one location to gather their opinions. If the training has been conducted in multiple sites in different geographic areas, it may be too expensive to evaluate all sites. You may decide to take a representative sample of trainees from the sites or concentrate on one site that everyone agrees is representative of the others.

Summary

- *Involve several people as evaluators: participants, line managers, and senior managers may have a valuable perspective.*

- *Consider setting up an evaluation committee or review board.*
- *To help you determine what to evaluate, go back to your training objectives.*
- *Consider a staged evaluation process to track trainees' progress over time.*
- *Determine where the evaluation will take place. Weigh the pros and cons of face to face contact with the trainees' at their work space versus a more distant approach such as surveys or questionnaires.*

Evaluation Design

Determining the evaluation design is one of the most important components of training evaluation. Most evaluation designs involve comparisons of the performance of trainees at various points in time, or comparisons of the trainees with a group of individuals who did not receive training. Five common designs are:

- the single measurement design
- the pre- and post-measurement with the same group
- the control group design
- the three group design
- the control group with a post test design.

The Single Measurement Design

This design takes a measurement of the effect of the training on participants at some point after the training.

The measurement might be a test, an observation of the participant's ability to perform a specific skill, or an interview to gain information on the participant's progress. The method is the least reliable of the four, but also the least complicated and easiest to administer. Measuring improvement of individuals and the organisation is more meaningful if you can obtain measurement of how individuals performed before the training. Single measurement programme designs are used when this pre-training measurement is not possible. In the case of training on brand new machinery, it would be illogical to obtain a measurement of performance before the training since it would be nil. Though desirable, logistics may also prevent you from obtaining a pre-training measurement.

Acuma Ltd., a U.K. financial services company, administers tests after technical training on products such as pensions, life assurance, and unit trusts. The pass rate and average scores on these computer based tests serve as one means to evaluate the overall effectiveness of the field training that precedes the tests. Reebok UK used the single measurement design in its two day leadership

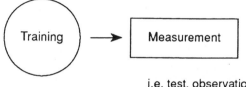

i.e. test, observation, interview or
other method.

Fig. 4.1   Single Measurement Design

course for middle and senior managers. The evaluation consisted of post course questionnaires and interviews with participants. Reebok discovered that 75% of participants felt the course would be useful to them in their work particularly in the areas of improved communication and motivation.

Pre- and Post-Training with the same Group Design

Unlike the single measurement design, this method takes a pre-training measurement of participants and compares it with a post-training measurement of the same group. In designing pre- and post-training designs it is important that the pre- and post-measures, tests for example, are identical or similar and are conducted under similar conditions. When knowledge or proficiency of a skill is obviously nil before a group undertakes training, it makes no sense to use this method. For example, there is little point in conducting a pre-test on acquisition of the French language if trainees have not spoken a word of French before the training.

Fig. 4.2   Pre- and Post-Training Design With The Same Group

Control Group Design

Unlike the single measurement programme design and the pre- and post-training design with the same group, the control group design introduces into the evaluation process a group who did not receive the training. This group, called the control group, is compared to the experimental group, the group of trainees. The most important part of this evaluation design is choosing two groups that are similar. For example, in comparing two groups of managers, one would want to ensure that both groups represented similar age groups, an equal percentage of men and women, the same departments, came from similar jobs, and had similar abilities. If care isn't taken in the early stages to select similar groups, the design will be flawed and the data inconclusive.

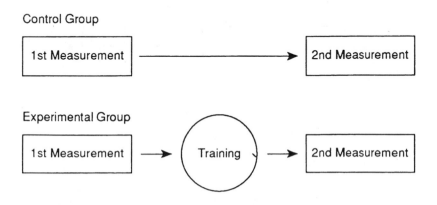

Fig. 4.3   Control Group Design

Three Group Design

The most reliable yet most complicated and difficult to administer design is a three group design. It controls for any effect that the pre-test may have had on participants. In addition, because it uses a control group, it isolates the effect of time. With time, performance or attitudes can change. Factors other than training may have caused a change in performance. If the pre- and post-measurements are the same for the control group, we know that these other factors are not responsible for any change in performance. In this design, a first group, a group of trainees, is given a pre-measurement, undergoes the training and is then given a post-measurement. A second group, the control group, is given both the pre- and post-measurements but receives no training. The third group, another group of the trainees, is trained identically to the first group of trainees and is measured after the training but is not given a pre-training measurement. If the post-measurements for the first and third groups are identical, we can assume that the pre-test did not influence the performance of trainees.

Control Group with a Post-Measurement

Sometimes logistically it is too difficult to administer a pre-test. In this design the control group is given only the post-measurement and compared with the group of trainees who are given the same post-measurement. Although this design is simpler to administer, the absence

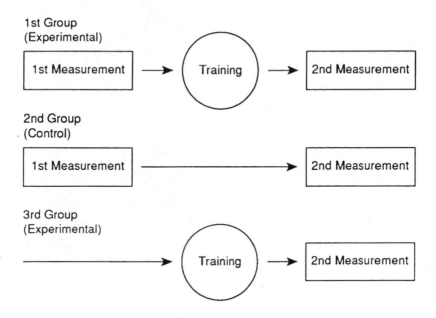

Fig. 4.4   Three Group Design

of a pre-test makes the effects of the training on the participants arguable. We cannot be certain that training caused the change in performance without a pre-measurement.

Lucas Aerospace, winner of the National Training Award, used the control group with a post-measurement design in determining the effect of 11 training modules on its graduate engineers. It compared the performance of two groups of graduates, one without the benefit of the training modules. Gathering data from several groups, including the participants and their managers, Lucas was able to make a case for the impact of training on its graduates. Interviews and informal discussions with

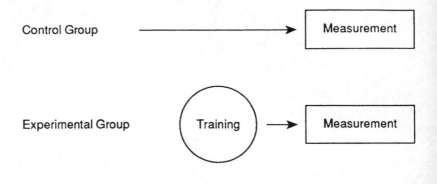

Fig. 4.5   Control Group With Post Measurement

managers of the trainee group indicated that the trainee group were better prepared and more able to do their jobs than their predecessors, the untrained group. In addition to the managers' opinions, Lucas used reports, called log book audits, from the graduates themselves. The second group of graduates felt better prepared. Retention rates between the two groups of graduates were compared. Seventeen individuals from the untrained group left the company while only one left the trained group. Exit interviews verified that the leavers left because of the culture shock after leaving university of hard work in the real world. The training modules addressed these work pressures by teaching time management and stress management. An independent body, The Institute of Electrical Engineers (IEE), although not part of the evaluation process, gave testimony to it. In its accreditation of engineers it reviewed the graduate training scheme and supported the findings of the evaluation.

In all control group designs, the control group should be randomly selected. This makes generalising about findings more acceptable.

Choosing a Sample

Sometimes the sheer number of individual trainees makes evaluating all of them unrealistic. Choosing a sample of them is a way around this problem. Care must be taken in selecting the sample and the number of people within the sample. The following methods are commonly used:

Random Sampling

Random sampling eliminates bias. One way of picking a random sample is to assign a number to each trainee and then generate a random computerised table of numbers. From the table, then choose the appropriate number of numbers beginning from the top left hand side of the table. For example, choose the first 20 numbers, if you intend to evaluate twenty people, or the first 50 numbers if you intend to evaluate 50 individuals. Finally, find the individuals who correspond to the numbers you have selected.

Stratified Random Sampling

The purpose of any sampling exercise is to obtain a representative sample of the entire group of trainees. When the training has been conducted with differing proportions of individuals from different departments (20 people from the marketing department, 50 people from the finance department, and 60 from the personnel department, for example), you should use a stratified random sampling technique. This method is just like random sampling but within the stratified groups. Assign the marketing group numbers, the finance department numbers and the personnel group numbers. Decide the percentage of trainees you want to evaluate and apply it across the board to each group. For example, if you want to evaluate 20% you would need to select 2 people from the marketing department, 10 people from the finance department, and 12 people from the personnel department. Now select the appropriate number of individuals from the computer generated list of random numbers.

Systematic Random Sampling

When you are dealing with very large populations, systematic random sampling may be useful. Assume you have a population of 1000 managers whom you have

trained. Evaluating all would be a very cumbersome process. With this technique, you would determine how many individuals you want to evaluate and divide 1000 by that number. For example, you may decide to evaluate 100 people (1000 ÷ 100 = 10). You would then put the 1000 individuals into 10 groups, each of 100 individuals. (Each individual would be assigned a number from 00 to 99.) From the first group you would apply random sampling techniques to choose 10 numbers. From the remaining nine groups, you would choose the same 10 numbers.

Cluster Sampling
Geography sometimes makes evaluating everyone an impossible task. If several sites received training and those sites are located across the country evaluating individuals from all sites may be impractical from a cost and resource point of view. In these cases, it is possible to select a number of sites rather than all of them. The sites should be randomly selected and the individuals within the chosen sites, randomly chosen. It is important that all sites are similar, if they are not, it could be argued that the sites that were chosen for the evaluation were not representative of the entire group.

Purposeful Sampling
Random sampling and cluster sampling are used when one wants to generalise from the sample population to the larger population. If one, on the other hand, wants to learn something about a specific group and is not concerned with generalising from the sample to the larger group, purposeful sampling is more appropriate. Let's

assume that decision makers in an organisation already know about the variation of performance across several office sites. They are more interested in finding out why "X" and "Y" offices are performing so poorly while "A" and "B" offices are doing well. An evaluation of these extreme cases (by comparing what makes individuals in the former offices do well and those in the latter do poorly) would prove more fruitful than taking a sample of individuals from all offices.

Deciding how many should be included in the sample

There is no easy answer to determining how many trainees to include in the evaluation exercise. If you have the time, money and energy and you decide it is possible, you may decide to include all of them. A few guidelines are helpful if you decide to choose a sample:

- If the population of trainees is small, the sample size must be larger in proportion to the total. As the population of trainees increases, the sample size in proportion to the whole decreases.
- The greater variation in the data, the larger the sample should be. For example, in training mechanics it might be determined that the variation in applying a skill is small; all mechanics seem to adjust the timing in cars in about the same way. The variation in conducting performance appraisals by managers, however, might be very large. The measure for variance, called standard deviation, can be obtained by applying a statistical formula to the population.
- Precision also effects the sample size. Through any

training exercise, one estimates the accuracy desired for a new prediction about performance. For example, it may be determined that the estimate for the amount of time mechanics take tuning cars be within 15 minutes of the actual new average to tune cars. The less precision, the larger the sample size needs to be.[†]

- Reliability of the estimate also helps determine the sample size. With any sample, it is possible that it doesn't reflect the real value. If one wants to be 95% sure that the sample reflects the larger population, the reliability (or confidence level) is said to be 95%. The higher the reliability desired, the larger the sample size needed.

Generally speaking, the sample size should be as large as is practically possible. A trained statistician should be consulted in the early stages of the evaluation project for advice on the sample size.

Summary

- *Choosing the evaluation design will depend on logistics and what you want to measure.*
- *Five common designs are: the single measurement, pre-post with the same group, control group, three group, and control group with a post-measurement design.*
- *You may consider taking a sample of your trainees if evaluating all of them is too big a task.*
- *Deciding on the sample size depends on three things: how big the entire population of trainees is, how varied you think what you are measuring them on is (attitude, knowledge, or skills), and how precise you want your prediction about their new performance to be.*

[†] Jack Phillips, *Training and Evaluation Methods*, p.370–1.

Collecting Data

If the evaluation design calls for some type of pre- and post-measurement of participants, it is critical to think about collecting data before the training exercise. This data tends to fall into one of two categories: hard or soft data.

Hard Data

Hard data includes those units of measurement that are easily quantifiable. In a survey of 100 organisations, hard data emerged as the most effective way of assessing the impact of training.[†] Hard data includes measurements about the output of work, the quality of the product or process, the savings in terms of time and money. A good

‡ Training Evaluation: An IRS Survey. *Employment Development Bulletin,* May 1992, p.4.

place to look for hard data measurements in your organisation is through the systems, sales and finance departments
or through a department that is leading a quality improvement project. A few examples of hard data are:

- items produced
- items sold
- applications processed
- downtime (for equipment)
- overtime
- error rates
- product defects
- time to complete a project or finish a task
- retention of staff rate
- training costs per employee

Soft Data

With many human resource training efforts, hard data
about performance may not be obtainable nor appropriate
as a measurement. For example, management training may
be concerned with changing managers' attitudes about their
role or in improving motivation. Measuring these types of
changes is different from measuring an easily quantifiable
production rate. Soft data include things such as work
habits, attitudes, new skills acquired, feelings, work climate
and culture. Soft data are often not as easy to measure
objectively. Changes in attitude, for example, can not be
measured with as much precision as downtime of equipment. Examples of soft data include:

- satisfied employees (employee morale)
- performance appraisal ratings

- communication skills
- perception of role
- attitude about promotional prospects
- number and nature of employee complaints
- counselling skills of managers
- perceived friendliness or professionalism of staff

In evaluating its management development programme, Shearings, a U.K. coach operator, used both hard and soft data in measuring pre- and post-training effects. Its hard data measures included direct sales which increased by an average of 5% and savings in wastage and costs per head. Its soft data measures included customer surveys that showed a decrease in dissatisfied customers and increased staff involvement.

Using Hard and Soft Data

In determining what type of data to use several questions have to be answered:

- What are the objectives of the training?
- At which level or levels are the training objectives? (reaction, learning, behaviour, result (organisational impact))
- How can I measure these objectives?
- How easy or difficult will it be to obtain the data?
- What will be an acceptable form of data? (For example, the organisation may only be interested in hard data as evidence of improvement.)
- Do I need to create evaluation tools or are they already present within the organisation?
- Am I looking for an improvement in a skill or behaviour that can only be measured by soft data?

Found Data

As you are putting together your evaluation design, you will need to ask yourself whether or not data already exists that could help you in evaluating the impact of training or whether or not you need to create your own tools. As you are putting together your evaluation design, it is worth asking individuals in other departments if measures exist that might be useful in evaluating the training. For example, in a prominent U.K. financial services company the sales and marketing group produced weekly statistics for salespeople on the effectiveness of their interactions with clients. These were measured by looking at the ratio of cold calls to appointments with prospects and by the ratio of first interviews with a prospect to closes on the product. These statistics were generated not only for the individual, but also for branch offices and for the entire sales force. The training department was able to take this "found data" and use it as an evaluation tool. Individuals' statistics were taken before training on telephone skills and closing in the interview and compared with their statistics after the training. The evaluators were able to look at pre-training averages on these skills for the entire salesforce compared with post-training averages on the same skills.

Summary

- *It is important to establish baseline data related to trainees' knowledge, skills, behaviours or attitudes if you intend to compare their pre-training and post-training results.*
- *Hard or soft data may be useful in your evaluation. Which type of data you use depends on what you are measuring and what is available in your organisation.*

6
Designing Questionnaires and Tests

Two of the most common evaluation tools are questionnaires and tests. Questionnaires are often used to collect participants' reactions to the training immediately afterward. Keep in mind that after-course questionnaires capture immediate feelings about the course but do not measure learning back on the job or organisational impact of the training. They are most helpful in modifying the content of the training, in understanding how well the training facilities met the group's expectations and in helping the trainers modify their presentation style.

The Pros and Cons of Questionnaires

Questionnaires are easy to administer and, if constructed well, are easy to analyse. One major drawback of after-course questionnaires is that they are self-reporting and, therefore, by their nature biased. They are most useful to collect reactions, perceptions and feelings. If, however, you want to collect information about participants' learning and skill level, a self-reporting questionnaire may not be the best evaluation tool.

Selecting the Question Type

After you've determined what you want to ask, you will need to decide on a question format. You may vary the question format, but try not to include too many styles or you may risk confusing the person filling out the question-naire. The following are common question formats:

- open-ended questions
- a checklist from which individuals check all those that apply
- a Yes/No or True/False format
- multiple choice questions
- ranking items in a list from most important to least important or from most satisfied to least satisfied

Tips for Constructing Questionnaires

1. When you develop the training, write a detailed training design or outline of what will be included in the training. Make sure that your questionnaire covers every major aspect of the training.

2. Ask questions about how well the objectives were covered. List the objectives on the questionnaire. Without this reminder, participants may not remember what the course objectives were.

3. Select the question format. In doing so consider how easy it will be to analyse the responses. Open-ended questions will be more difficult to analyse than multiple choice style questions.

4. Always include detailed instructions about how to fill out the questionnaire. Give an example of how to fill out one question so that, for example, individuals see that they are to tick a box or fill in a square to indicate their response.

5. Avoid asking two questions within one question. For example, "How valuable was the information about active listening skills and handling performance discussions to you?" asks two distinct questions. If a rating scale of 5 to 1 were applied to the question, the individual answering the question may feel that active listening skills was very valuable, a "5", while handling performance discussions was not as valuable, a "3". The question forces the individual to give only one response to two different subject areas.

6. Many questionnaires include multiple choice type questions that use a scale with numbers that correspond to values. Consider carefully the scale that you choose and the number of responses you make available. You may want to use a scale that asks about level of satisfaction, importance, relevance to job, ability or performance. If you assign a level of satisfaction, for example, to a series of numbers on a scale, make sure that the scale is not too large. It would not make sense to use a 10 point scale in the following example:

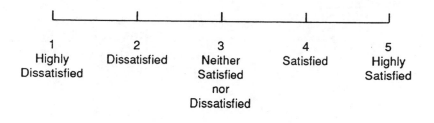

1	2	3	4	5
Highly Dissatisfied	Dissatisfied	Neither Satisfied nor Dissatisfied	Satisfied	Highly Satisfied

Fig. 6.1

If, on the other hand, you want to use a 10 point scale to give individuals more freedom to choose a value, simply assign the level of satisfaction to the two extreme values.

1	2	3	4	5	6	7	8	9	10
Very Dissatisfied									Very Satisfied

Fig. 6.2

7. After you have written the questionnaire, pilot it with several individuals to determine if they understand the questions and to judge whether or not the length of the questionnaire is appropriate. Re-word, delete or add questions based on the feedback from the pilot.

The Alternative Travel Group in Oxford have used customer questionnaires in evaluating its staff and its training. An intensive training course, mandatory for all trip leaders and managers, covers job competencies such as management of people, managing trip logistics, dealing with

difficult situations, conflict resolution, and social skills. Areas covered on the 52 point questionnaire include: management of the trip, punctuality, background knowledge of the country being visited, sociability and friendliness, contribution to the enjoyment of the individual's holiday – all things that can be traced back to the training.

The Use of Tests

There are several ways to test whether or not participants understood the material from a training course and whether or not they are able to apply their knowledge. First, consider what you are interested in evaluating. Are you interesting in evaluating participants':

- recall of information?
- comprehension or understanding of ideas?

- ability to do something or apply knowledge?
- ability to analyse complex information?

The style of questions you ask should test the participants' level of understanding in which you are interested. Multiple-choice style questions often test recall of information, but may also test one's ability to solve complex problems such as mathematical ones. True/False style questions are often used to test recall of facts and the ability to make inferences. Essay style questions often require individuals to demonstrate their understanding of ideas and also their ability to analyse and synthesise information.

Skill and Performance Tests/Job Simulations

A departure from pen and paper tests are tests that uncover a participants' ability to do something. A skill or performance test might involve an evaluator observing an individual perform a job task or conduct a roleplay exercise. Examples of performance tests include pilot flight simulations in which pilots demonstrate their ability to land aircraft in emergency situations or memo and letter writing where participants demonstrate their practical application of communication skills after a business writing course.

Performance or skill tests, roleplays, or job simulations need to be carefully designed. Instructions should be the same for every participant. This is particularly important if they are given verbally. Evaluators should use standard observation critique sheets to ensure that they are scoring each individual against the same criteria. Observation critique sheets are explained in more detail in chapter 7.

Criterion versus Norm Referenced Tests

Tests scores need to be evaluated or compared against some

standard. Norm referenced tests compare participants to each other or to a larger norm group. These tests are useful if you want to select out the "highest" and "lowest" performing individuals or groups. Commercial tests are often norm referenced; an individual's test scores are compared to the average for another group. The group might be graduates, managers, non-managers, or an occupational group such as salespeople, for example.

Criterion referenced tests determine a cut-off for acceptable performance. On a test with 100 questions, the cut-off might be 80 or it might be 60, depending on the difficulty of the test and the decision of the test designers. Acuma, a financial services company in the United Kingdom, uses criterion referenced tests to determine whether or not an individual passes or fails its computer-based product training. A minimum score of 80% is required to pass.

Test Anxiety

One threat to the validity of tests is participants' potential test anxiety. One way to diminish the effects of test anxiety is to explain that the purpose of the test is to evaluate the programme not specific individuals.

Summary

- *Decisions regarding test design include:*
  - *the question format*
  - *length of test*
  - *level of difficulty*
  - *comparison or norm group used*
- *Decisions regarding questionnaire design include:*
  - *the question format and scale*

– *the instructions*
– *matching the questionnaire to the course objectives*
- *Criterion-referenced tests determine a minimum acceptable level of performance or cut-off point (e.g. 70%)*
- *Norm-referenced tests compare the individual to a target group with similar characteristics as the individual.*

Qualitative Evaluation Methods

The Characteristics of Qualitative Methods

Qualitative data provide depth, breadth, and detailed accounts of how individuals perceived an event or a programme. These methods are useful when the evaluator wants to know how participants' experienced a programme. Questionnaires with standardised items are valuable for analysing large amounts of information, but often they do not help the evaluator understand why something is the way it is. For example, if 50% of individuals responding to a training questionnaire indicate that the programme was not relevant to their job, the evaluator still does not know why. Open-ended, detailed responses via interviews might reveal problems the questionnaire did not uncover. For example, one participant of a communications training course might have said the following:

> 'Although I think the training was relevant, my boss does not. I am discouraged from taking time out of my day to deal with people issues. I'm told not to take my eye off the production line.'

Another might have said

> 'Our area is organised so that none of us has the ultimate responsibility for communication. I think it is important and relevant to my job, but I don't feel I should take the lead. My workmates might feel I am trying to overstep my bounds.'

Qualitative evaluation techniques provide a descriptive account of the impact of the training that may be very useful along side quantitative approaches. Verbatim comments from participants evoke emotion in others. Sometimes they help sell the idea of additional training. These are typical comments from board members of a large corporation after reading personal accounts:

- 'I didn't realise until now just how important the training was to these people. They obviously feel the content was terrific and they built trust with their work colleagues over the 5 days.'

- 'We really do need to do something about the training facilities. They clearly detract from what we are trying to teach. It seems everyone feels our training rooms are substandard and our equipment neolithic.'

– 'These comments bring out the desperate need for better communication between managers and their employees. We need to think about putting some resources toward this issue.'

Types of Qualitative Methods

The most common types of qualitative evaluation methods used in organisations include:

- observations
- interviews
- focus groups
- case studies
- action plans
- performance appraisals

Observations

Observations are valuable to the evaluator for the simple reason that they capture what other methods do not. An observation will help the evaluator determine whether or not a skill can be applied to the workplace. An interview with the individual or a self-reporting style questionnaire may not be as reliable as actually watching an individual to determine his or her level of proficiency. In addition, the observer may be able to spot something that participants routinely overlook about their own behaviour. Finally, participants may be reluctant to say in interviews that which might be easily picked up in an observation. For example, after a teambuilding training exercise participants may be reluctant to say that they feel one colleague reacts defensively in meetings while another dominates conversation. An observer of the meeting, however, may be able to see instances where one reacts defensively and the other monopolizes conversation.

To Observe or not to Observe?

Some skills or subject areas are highly emotional or political. One always needs to ask, "Will I alienate staff by observing this skill?" "Will this person feel terribly uncomfortable if I observe them?" Observing performance appraisal discussions to evaluate managers' skills may be considered an invasion of privacy. Observing individuals operating machinery, however, may be the best way to evaluate whether or not they have learned the necessary skills and may not offend anyone.

OCCUPATIONAL HAZARD.
HE'S AN OBSERVER.

Behaviour Checklist versus Non-Structured Observations

There are two common methods of observations: the behaviour checklist method and the non-structured observation. With the former method, the observer uses a checklist to guide him or her in observing specific actions, skills, and behaviours of the participant. In this case, the evaluator knows exactly what he or she is looking for. This method has its advantages because the notes from the observation are easy to analyse.

With the non-structured approach, the evaluator conducts the observation with a blank notepad. Essentially, he or she attempts to write down everything that happens during the observation including what is said by whom and any actions or non-verbal gestures that are made. After several observations are done, the evaluator looks for themes, patterns of behaviour, and patterns of activity among them. For example, from observation data of new supervisors conducting staff meetings with employees an evaluator discovered that more than half of the supervisors exhibited gestures and speech that showed a lack of confidence – closed body language, a wavering voice and lack of eye contact. In addition, the same group of supervisors seemed to have lost control of the meeting; people came in late and left early and individuals showed a lack of respect for the supervisors by continually interrupting.

The non-structured approach is difficult to master and harder to analyse than the behaviour checklist approach. It can, however, uncover elements of behaviour that will be missed by the checklist approach. The checklist is limited by what can be conceived by the evaluator before the observation. The non-structured approach is useful when evaluators want to discover information about a training programme and may not know exactly what they are looking for.

Designing a Structured Observation with a Behaviour Checklist

The success of a structured observation using a checklist depend on a thoughtfully designed checklist. When designing an observation checklist keep these points in mind:

■ Checklist categories should be a reflection of the stated training objectives and should reflect important attributes for successful completion of an activity.

■ Each category should be distinct from another. The evaluator should provide an observer's guide that would highlight specifically what is being looked for in each category. This ensures that multiple evaluators are judging against the same criteria.

■ Where behaviours should be practiced in some sort of sequence, the observation checklist should reflect this sequence. Finally, avoid categories that elicit personality characteristics or subjective information. Looking for "friendliness" implies a personality characteristic, whereas observing whether or not a manager smiles and greets an individual focuses on behaviour.

■ Try not to include too many categories in one observation. Remember that observation requires acute awareness of what is going on. Observers may not be able to concentrate on watching for too many behaviours.

■ Include negative behaviours. For example, when observing a manager conducting a meeting with an employee, it

Sample Behaviour Checklist

Skill: Interviewing
Length of Observation: 45 minutes
Observer's Name: . . . .
Check all that apply and supply relevant evidence of behaviour.
The Introduction to the Interview:
The manager . . . (yes or no)   *Comment*
. . . . . . introduced himself.
. . . . . . briefly described the company
         and its history.
. . . . . . asked the individual to hold
         his/her questions until the end.
During the Interview:
The manager . . . (yes or no)
. . . . . . followed the interview script.
. . . . . . maintained good eye contact.
. . . . . . asked leading questions.
. . . . . . took notes.
. . . . . . controlled the pace of the interview.
. . . . . . maintained control of the interview.
. . . . . . allowed the interviewee to dominant.
         (interviewee went off on tangents)
. . . . . . asked the individual if he/she had
         questions.
. . . . . . avoided asking questions that produced
         hypothetical answers (If you were . . .)
. . . . . . maintained positive body language
         (open posture; relaxed rather than stiff)
At the end of the interview:
The manager . . . (yes or no)
. . . . . . explained "next steps".
. . . . . . thanked the individual.
Rate the overall effectiveness of the interviewer, placing a tick mark on the
appropriate description.
. . . . . . **Excellent**
. . . . . . **Very Good**
. . . . . . **Average** (some additional training required)
. . . . . . **Poor** (more training required)

might be useful to ask if the manager 'over controls' the meeting by discouraging dialogue.

Opposite is an example of an observation checklist for assessing managers' ability to conduct an interview.

Observing the Frequency of Behaviour

Sometimes the evaluator wants to document how often a trainee practices a particular behaviour or group of behaviours over a given period of time. At Acuma Ltd., a U.K. financial services company, trainers observe how often financial consultants ask potential clients "open", "closed" and "reflective" questions. The ability to ask these types of questions is something that is drilled relentlessly during a sales training workshop. Acuma have developed an observation checklist to track how many open, closed, and reflective questions the financial consultant asks during an interview with the client. This checklist, used during practice and roleplay sessions, offers a useful tool to see how well the trainee has progressed since the workshop. It helps the training department monitor the success of its training, but also assists the financial consultant and the financial consultant's manager in tracking his or her improvement.

Participant–Observer or Complete Observer?

Evaluators need to decide if they are complete outsiders as evaluators, not having participated in any of the training or whether they are participants and observers. The participant–observer has the advantage of an insider's point

Key Money Concerns/Data Gathering
Drill-for-Skill Feedback Form

Planner name	Open Probe	Reflect. Probe	Closed Probe	Commit-ment	Comments
Fred	II		I		+ Eye contact
Ben			IIII		+ Use of name − Watch driver style, open up dialogue w/open probes
Nancy	II	I	II		Hesitant but articulate, work on smoother flow
Paul	II			I	+ 4 M's
Tom	I		I		− Pay more attention, listen
Ben			II		− Gathered facts only, Use open probes to paint the picture
Lori	II	I			+ Focused on feelings created urgency

Note: "+" means well done", "−" means "needs improvement".

* Courtesy of Acuma Ltd. (U.K), and IDS Financial Services (U.S.A.)

Feedback Guidelines

During a *Key Money Concerns* drill-for-skill, look for and provide feedback on the planner's ability to:

Uncover Feelings – using Open Probes

Show Understanding/Summarize – using Reflective Probes

Create Urgency – using Open and Closed Probes

Gain Commitment – using Closed Probes

Determine the right time to close – listen for buying signals

Listening carefully

Adjust to Social Style – 4 M's
  Meet eyes
  Match mood
  Mirror body language
  Model representational system

Handle resistance effectively

During a *Date Gathering* drill-for-skill, look for and provide feedback on the planner's ability to:

Gather Facts – use Closed Probes

Uncover Feelings and Create Urgency – use Open Probes

Gain Commitment – use Closed Probes

Listen carefully

Adjust to Social Style – 4 M's
  Meet eyes
  Match mood
  Mirror body language
  Model representational system

Handle resistance effectively

of view and will have a better understanding of the programme and the emotions of those within it. The participant–observers must determine whether or not to disclose the fact that they are evaluators. In some cases, evaluators are able to obtain more interesting and reliable data if their role is kept secret. Complete observers may be more objective than participant–observers because of their lack of involvement in the training.

Using Videotaped Observations

Sometimes because of logistics observing individuals in person is impossible. Under certain circumstances, you might ask them to send you a copy of a videotape featuring the skill that you want to evaluate. Giving clear instructions to participants is essential. Do you want an unrehearsed example of something or their best effort? One clear advantage of using video is the replay feature; the evaluator can look at the tape several times to pick up the participant's behaviours. In addition to their use in evaluation of training, videotapes can be used as a coaching tool with individuals after the training.

Potential Problems with Observations

Several problems with observations stem from the fact that human nature interfers with the methodology. The evaluator should be aware of the following tendencies:

The Halo Effect

Evaluators also have the tendency to carry over a rating from one category to another in an effort to portray the individual as consistent. For example, one might assess one category as "very good" based on solid evidence. That assessment of "very good" may carry over to the next category in spite of the fact that the individual exhibited "average" performance.

Avoidance of Extremes

Most raters stay away from the extremes on any rating scale. Evaluators tend to rate individuals using more average categories such as "average", "very good" rather than "excellent" or "very poor". This type of error is sometimes referred to as an error of central tendency.

Generosity Error

In a study of supervisors and their employees, Kingstrom and Maidstone (1985) found that those individuals who had a high level of personal relationship and task efficiency received higher ratings than those without a high level of personal relationship. The personal acquaintance factor seemed to have a predictive link to higher ratings. Evaluators may overestimate positive qualities of those individuals with whom they are well acquainted.

Fundamental Attribution Error

An evaluator may label an individual based on one observation. This stereotyping of behaviour may not be accurate. For example, an individual being observed may be extremely nervous and may be labelled as "anxiety ridden" when this is not the true under most circumstances. It is best to observe individuals more than once to ensure that the behaviour witnessed is an accurate representation of how the person behaves in most situations.

Personal Frame of Reference

Individual raters observing the same individual may come

up with different opinions of what the ratings should be. Some individuals will place more emphasis and importance on one skill and another, more emphasis on a different skill.

Tips For Effective Observations and for Handling These Problems:

1. The best way to handle these problems is by coaching evaluators. Make evaluators aware of these tendencies and practice evaluations so that you can discuss individual ratings. Give them constructive feedback on their observation skills.

2. Determine what you want observers to look for and coach them in effective note taking.

3. Videotape an example of the behaviour they will observe correctly demonstrated.
4. Try to keep observations relatively short. It is difficult to observe people over even one hour.
5. To put the individual at ease explain how the observation data will be used. Many participants will be more comfortable knowing the data will be aggregated and knowing they will remain anonymous.
6. Make sure that evaluators are not observing individuals whom they know very well or with whom they are friends.

Interviews

While we can use observations to find out how well someone does something, interviews capture individual's thoughts and feelings about a training course or programme. The purpose of interviewing is to find out another individual's perspective.

Types of Interviews

The Informal Conversational Interview

This type of interview is often part of a participant–observer situation in which the participant–observer engages individuals in the training programme in conversation about the training. Participants are often unaware of the fact that they are being interviewed. The conversation flows naturally from the context of the situation in which the individuals find themselves. The evaluator does not know what he or she will ask nor what he or she will find out. The evaluator takes notes after the conversation about what he or she learned.

The Interview Guide Approach

Another method of interviewing is to prepare an interview guide with basic topics to be covered. The interviewer is given a list of questions or topics to cover but is free to develop the conversation and to word questions in his or her own way. This format allows the interviewer to be flexible and conversational, yet cover all of the topics. Analysing data from the interview guide and the informal, conversational interview will be more difficult than analysing data from a rigidly structured interview. The results, however, may yield data that otherwise would have been overlooked.

The Structured, Standardised Interview

At the other extreme from the informal, conversational interview is the structured, standardised interview. The evaluator writes a series of carefully worded questions that will be asked in a specific order, exactly as they are written. The standardised interview does not allow spontaneity, but it does have these advantages:

- decision makers can see exactly what questions will be asked of each participant in the training programme.
- if several people are interviewing, the variation of their approach will be minimized.
- the data will be easy to categorise and analyse.
- the interviewer can stay focused and will know exactly what needs to be covered in the time allowed.

Questions

In determining what to ask in an interview think about how an interview differs from other evaluation methods. It uncovers attitudes, opinions, feelings, one's experiences and thoughts about the training exercise. Interviews may not be the best vehicle for determining the skill level mastered. Common questions that could be asked include:

- Have you used information from the training course now that you are back on the job? Why or why not?
- What did you find the most (least) helpful part of the training? Why?
- What is your opinion of the course content?
- What were your overall feelings about the course?

Introduce the Interview

Before you begin asking questions, briefly explain why you are conducting the interview, how you will use the information, the confidentiality of the interview, and the interview format. If you don't take the time to set the stage, you may not have the individual's full cooperation and attention.

Avoid Leading Questions

Leading questions are often subtle. Interviewers may not be aware that they are asking leading questions. Consider the difference between these sets of questions, "How valuable did you find the training?" versus "What is your opinion of the training?" Or "Describe how you are currently using the training on the job" versus "Are you using the training on the job? Why or why not?" In the first example, the first question frames the individual's thinking by describing the training as possibly "valuable". The second question is truly open-ended in that it does not guide the person in any particular direction. In the second example, the statement is biased from the start by assuming that the training is being used on the job. It is far better to ask "If" the training is being used rather than "How" the training is being used.

Avoid Questions that ask more than one thing

As with questionnaires, avoid questions that ask more than one thing or questions that ask a series of things. The statement, "Give me your opinions about the course instructor, the venue, the length of the programme and the course content," will be difficult for the participant to follow. He or she may end up focusing on only part of the question, probably the latter part.

Allow the Participant to Give You Negative Information

There is an art to giving an individual permission to respond with negative information. The art comes from practising your question format. Consider the impact of this question, "Some of the participants found the programme to be of little use, some said they felt it was over their heads, some found it somewhat useful, while others found it extremely valuable. What was your experience with the programme?" The question demonstrates that a range of responses is acceptable and that the evaluator will not be surprised by any type of response. Where you think an individual might feel uncomfortable giving negative information, demonstrate that a range of responses from negative to positive is possible. If the individual gives you negative information, do not act surprised.

Frame Questions

By using a short sentence before a question, you can help prepare the individual to answer it. For example, the simple sentence, "Now I'd like you to think about how the training could be improved", before the question "What would you do differently if you were teaching the course?" can help prepare the individual to answer the question.

Ask for Clarification on Judgemental Words

Certain adjectives have a variety of interpretations determined by the speaker. Words such as "good", "terrible", "useless", "excellent", "success" and "failure" are open to interpretation. Ask the interviewee what he or she means by "successful". Find out what the individual felt was "terrible" and what was "good".

The Logistics of Interviewing

Try to hold all of the interviews under similar circumstances. Determine if the interviews will be in your office, a conference room or the work space of the interviewee. Choose a setting that will be comfortable for the interviewee and one that will be free of distractions. Ensure that each interview is the same length of time.

Focus Groups

Focus groups are small group discussions to find out how individuals perceive a programme. A trained facilitator asks a few thought provoking, open-ended questions and records the responses of individuals in the group either by using a taperecorder or by taking notes. The focus group is an efficient alternative to the interview when the questions that need to be asked are not of a sensitive nature and people are willing to be open in a group setting.

Tips for Running Focus Groups Sessions

■ Keep the group fairly small, between 6 and 10 people. The group should be large enough to generate discussion, but small enough so that everyone participates.

■ Use a trained facilitator. A facilitator should remain neutral and be able to manage the discussion so that everyone participates. He or she will know when to let the conversation digress into something that is relevant to the topic and when to pull the conversation back on track.

■ If you have the resources, it is useful to have two facilitators, one to concentrate on the group dynamics and managing the discussion and one to write down verbatim what individuals say.

■ Brief the organisation and participants before the focus group. Let senior members of the organisation know what you are doing so that you have their blessing and their support. Brief participants via a memo or telephone call, explaining the purpose of the session and how you intend to use the information.

■ If you have three important topic areas or questions to ask, divide your time up into thirds and watch the clock so that you don't short change one important question.

■ Determine what percentage of the trainees will participate in the focus group discussions. Use one of the sampling strategies, described in Chapter 4, to ensure that the individuals selected for the focus groups are representative of the rest of the trainees.

Analysing Focus Group Data

Analysing focus group data is similar to analysing interview data. Look for themes or patterns of responses that form a picture of the experiences of the trainees. As you are going through the focus group notes, it is helpful to use codes in the margins of your notes to help categorise the data. For example, if you were analysing data about a communications training course you might use the letter "A" to denote anything that has to do with problems between a boss and subordinate, the letter "B" to denote problems with non-verbal communication, the letter "C" to denote written communication issues, and so on. After you have coded all of your notes, you can easily group comments together.

Case Studies

Case studies are useful as an evaluation methodology for examining extreme cases. Case studies are most often used to find the answers to "how" and "why" questions. Perhaps a training department wants to find out how the training has been used in "X" division, the highest performing division in the company, and compare this to how the training has been used in "Y" division, the lowest performing division in the country. Case studies will often reveal additional information that may not be related to the training programme, but which may be very useful to know. For example, in the former example, the evaluators may discover that "X" division's organisational structure is more streamlined than "Y" division's. This structural difference, in addition to how they've used the training, contributed to its success.

Stating Propositions

Once you have determined the "how" or "why" question you want to investigate, you need to state propositions, or probable reasons, related to your questions. For example, the propositions to the question about why "X" division is performing better than "Y" division might include:

- Individuals in "X" division apply the training in their day to day work.
- Managers reinforce the training with follow-up.
- People in the office talk about the training.
- The head of the division supports training in a visible way.
- The culture in "X" division supports the idea of continuous improvement and self-development.

Evaluators now spend time gathering evidence to either support or refute these propositions.

Collecting Data for the Case Study

In the former example, relevant data for the above case study might be interviews with trainees, training records kept in the divisions, interviews with the leaders of the divisions, internal correspondence and message boards that might support or neglect to mention the training programme, observations, the presence or absence of individual self development plans. As one is collecting data for a case study, additional propositions may be brought forward.

Defining the Unit of Analysis

To ensure the case study is manageable it is important to define the unit of analysis as the training programme. Resist the temptation to try to study the entire "X" division or "Y" division and focus on only those things that are relevant to the training. Discipline yourself to collect data that relates to the training programme and not superfluous information.

Linking the Data to the Propositions

Once the data is collected you can try to link it to your propositions. For example, you may find that two pieces of evidence (the division newsletter, a meeting with employees) support the fact that the leader of "X" division visibly supports the training and two other pieces of data (interviews and observations) support the premise that managers encourage follow-up to the training.

Presenting the Case Study

An individual reading the findings from the case study should be able to follow your trail of evidence that strongly supports your conclusions about how "X" and "Y" divisions used or did not use the training programme to make their division more or less successful.

One method of organising your finding would include the following:

- **Your research questions**. For example, you would explain that you want to find out whether "X" division is using the training differently than "Y" division, whether follow-up in the two divisions is different, and whether the leader's and managers' involvement in the training is different in the two divisions.
- **A description of the two divisions**: the structures, the number of employees, the locations, the leaders etc.
- **Your methodology**. For example, you would explain the data collection methods you used.
- **Your findings**.
- **An appendix with support for your findings**. This might

include example interview formats that were used, summaries of observations that were done, etc.

When not to use the Case Study Approach

If the organisation is interested in questions that deal with "how many" or "how much", the case study approach is not the appropriate methodology. In this case, it is better to use a survey instrument or a pre- and post-test. For example, if you want to find out whether and how much each individual improved his or her performance as a result of the training, a pre- and post-test is the best method. A questionnaire will tell you how many people felt the programme was valuable.

Action Plans

Action plans are becoming a more common way of measuring the impact of training in organisations. Evaluators typically look at action plans of trainees to monitor the degree to which they are implementing the training on the job. Two multinational corporations, American Express and Philips are using action plans to evaluate their training and help track the progress of individuals. American Express is tracking manager's progress in implementing concepts from leadership training. Via an action planning format, Philips ensures that participants understand the course objectives before they attend the training, record the actions that they propose to take when they return to work, and record the participant's action six months after the training. Philips ensures the authenticity of the action plan by two levels of review: one by the individual's immediate manager and one by the personnel or training specialist.

This two level review process helps control what otherwise might be a subjective assessment of performance improvement, an opinion held only by the trainee.

Action plans may also give the evaluator information about why individuals did not complete their action plans. In other words, the evaluator may find out important information about obstacles to the training process.

Performance Reviews

Performance reviews can be used to evaluate the impact of training, but they may prove to be too cumbersome. Appraisals can be analysed as a pre- and post-training measurement to see if individuals have improved a skill or behaviour that was taught in the training session. In determining whether or not the methodology is a sound one, the evaluator should examine several performance reviews to see whether or not managers supply detailed information about their employees. If the managers supply vague comments such as "employee needs to improve his communication skills" or "employee needs to improve technical ability", the appraisals will be unreliable. The evaluator would find it difficult to interpret what the manager meant by "communication skills" or "technical ability". If, on the other hand, the appraisal form elicits very specific information related to the training and managers use vocabulary consistently across the company, the appraisal method may work. For example, if an appraisal form highlights ten aspects of communication and everyone knows exactly what these labels mean, using appraisals to measure an improvement in communication skills would be useful.

Summary

- *Qualitative methods provide depth, breadth and detailed accounts of trainees' experiences.*
- *Common qualitative methods include: observations, interviews, focus groups, case studies, action plans, and performance appraisals.*
- *Observations may be structured (using a behaviour checklist) or unstructured.*
- *Interview types range from very structured to completely unstructured. The method you use depends on the amount of freedom you want to give the interviewee in answering questions.*
- *A focus group is a small group discussion with trainees on areas of interest to the evaluator.*
- *Case studies are usually in-depth analyses to find out "how" or "why" a particular group is performing very well or very badly.*
- *Action plans and performance reviews are useful methods for measuring changes in knowledge, skills, behaviours and attitudes.*

8

Quantitative Evaluation Methods

Many organisations are interested in hard, statistical measures to back up the perceived value of training. Statistics help describe the data and allow the evaluator to make inferences about the group being studied. The training department that wants to quantify data using statistics would be wise to keep the statistics simple so that they and others can understand them. It never hurts to ask the advice of a trained statistician in determining and developing the approaches that you use.

Computers can be immensely useful in generating statistics. Formulas exist for all statistics and can be computed by hand. However, computer software programmes exist that can make the computations far easier (see list of useful addresses at the end of this book). In addition to running the statistical formulas software packages on the market contain useful graphics to visually explain the effect of training on participants. The training specialist need not know how to calculate the statistics but should know the general principles behind those statistics that are useful in understanding the effects of training on trainees.

The Value of Using Statistics

1. Statistics help summarise large amounts of information.
2. Statistics help show relationships between two variables, training and improved performance, for example.
3. Statistics help show the difference in performance between a non-trained group and a trained group.

Summarising Information

Information about the performance of trainees before and after a training event can be summarised by means of a frequency or group frequency distribution. Each trainee is given a number. Trainees scores on a test given before the training are listed in one column and their scores on the same or similar test after the training in another column.

FREQUENCY DISTRIBUTIONS

Employee Number	% accuracy on performance management test BEFORE TRAINING	% accuracy on performance management test AFTER TRAINING
1	60	75
2	50	75
3	75	82
4	80	85
5	62	76
6	67	80
7	71	82
8	65	75
9	52	74
10	83	95
11	81	90
12	71	80
13	64	74
14	73	84
15	72	84

Fig. 8.1   Frequency Distribution

Perhaps a more useful way of summarising trainees' pre- and post-training performance is to establish intervals or ranges of performance and specify how many trainees fall within these intervals or ranges. This method, a group frequency, is illustrated below:

Frequency Histograms

Histograms, or bar charts, can be useful in graphically representing the information from a group frequency. The impact of trainee improvement is often more dramatically characterized by something visual such as a histogram. The

---

PUTTING A FREQUENCY DISTRIBUTION INTO RANGES

Intervals – % accuracy on Performance Management Test	No of employees before training	No. of employees after training
51 – 60%	3	0
61 – 70%	4	0
71 – 80%	6	8
81 – 90%	2	6
91 – 100%	0	1

* Putting scores in ranges helps show the most common range of scores (central tendency) and also show the general distribution of scores.

Fig. 8.2   Group Frequency

histogram will quickly show where the bulk of scores fall and the variation in the sample.

Measures of Central Tendency: Mean, Median and Mode

At times it is useful to locate a trainee's scores on a pre- or post-test within the distribution of all scores of trainees. One can compare the trainee's score with the mean, median and mode.

Mean

The mean, the average score, is computed by adding up all the scores and dividing by the number of scores. Although finding the mean for a group of scores is useful, it can be misleading as well. Extreme scores either very high or very low scores, will give a misleading picture of the group of trainees. For example, assume five trainees' scores are 10, 10, 9, 3, 2, and 1. The average or mean score of the group is 7 yet no one in the distribution scored a 7.

Median

The median score is the score corresponding to the 50th percentile; half of the scores fall above and half below the median. In the following group of scores the median is 8: 10, 10, 10, 9, 8, 5, 4, 2, 1. Eight stands half way between all of the values. The median is useful as a further description of the distribution of scores when the average is affected by extreme scores.

Mode

The mode is the most frequent score in a distribution. When the mean, median and mode are all at about the same

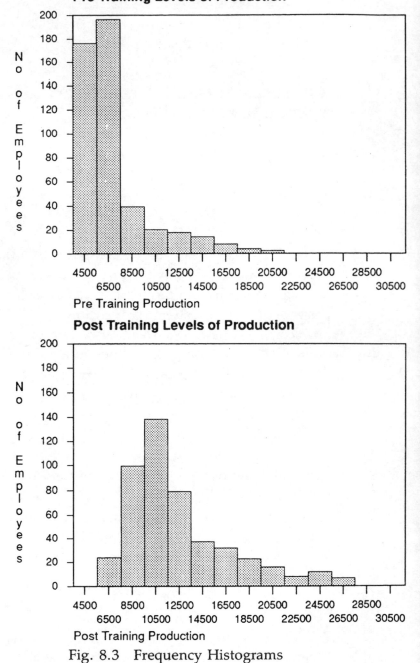

Fig. 8.3   Frequency Histograms

value the distribution is said to be a "normal or bell shaped" distribution.

Variability of The Data

Variability explains how spread out scores are from one another. High variability in a set of scores means the scores are very scattered and low variability means they are all similar. Training evaluators need to understand the concept of variability because it influences the precision with which inferences can be made about a group of trainees being studied. A high variability in the test scores of trainees, for example, would make it more difficult to be precise about the average trainee's performance.

Standard Deviation

One way of measuring the variability of scores is to calculate the standard deviation. Standard deviation looks at how variable scores are from the average or mean score. Extremely deviant scores will be far away from the mean. The standard deviation of a highly variable group of trainees may be 3 or 4, while the standard deviation for a group of trainees with low variability may be 1.5. In a normal or bell shaped distribution the standard deviation is approximately 2. About 95% of all scores fall within two standard deviations of the mean.

The examples on page 88 illustrate three groups of trainees: one with high variability, one with average variability (a normal distribution) and one with low variability.

Calculating Variability

The formula for calculating the standard deviation can be found in any elementary book on statistics. There are

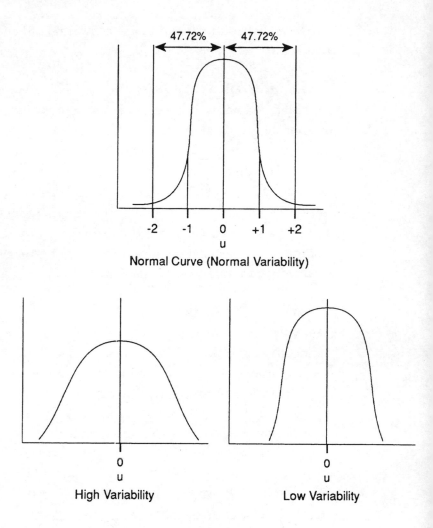

Fig. 8.4

several low cost software packages on the market that will do the calculation for you.

The Range

A more rudimentary way of estimating the variability of a

group of scores is to look at the range. The range is simply the largest score minus the smallest score. For example, assume the highest score on a post-test with trainees was 95 and the lowest score, 50; the range would be 45. A larger number usually reflects more variability. Range can be misleading when extreme values in a group of scores are not typical of the total variation. It should be used only as a rough estimate when standard deviation is not available.

Describing the Relationship between two Variables

Suppose you think training given to managers on disciplinary techniques and the effect of absenteeism has a bearing on actual absentee rates. You are interested in finding out if there is a relationship between the training and absentee rates. Did the absentee rate fall after the training took place? In another instance, you may want to find out if the current performance level is related to recent training on how to operate machinery. In statistical terms, you are interested in finding out if a correlation exists between training and absenteeism and between training and performance. In both cases, it is necessary to give the trainees some type of knowledge test to determine the extent to which the training might have had an impact on either performance or the absenteeism rates.

Plotting Scores on a Scatter Diagram

To see if a relationship exists between the two variables a range of values are plotted on what is called a scattergram. Test Scores are plotted against absenteeism and performance levels in the two examples. In the first example, the training department found that high test scores seemed to

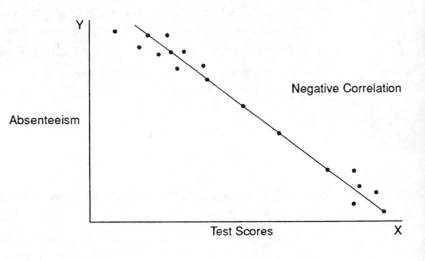

Fig . 8.5

predict low absentee rates among staff while low test scores demonstrated higher absentee rates. In the second example, high test scores suggested higher production levels while lower test scores indicated lower production levels.

In the first example, absenteeism is said to be "negatively correlated" with test scores because the pattern of the line of absentee rates and tests slopes down from left to right on the scattergram. In the second example, productivity is said to be "positively correlated" with test scores because the pattern of the line of productivity and test scores travels up from left to right on the scattergram.

If no relationship were to exist between the variables of test scores and productivity, the scattergram would indicate scores without a linear pattern.

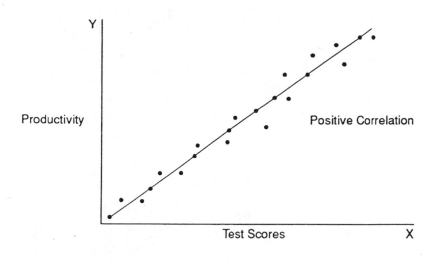

Fig. 8.6

The Degree of Correlation

The degree of the relationship is expressed numerically by the correlation coefficient. When there is no relationship between variables the correlation coefficient is "o". When a perfect positive correlation exists the correlation coefficient is +1. When a perfect negative correlation exists the correlation coefficient is −1. Anything in between +1 and −1 would indicate the strength of the correlation. Roughly speaking, a weak positive correlation would be between +0.2 and +0.4. Anything between a +0.2 and −0.2 would probably indicate that a relationship does not exist. A strong positive correlation would be between +0.7 and +1. A strong negative correlation would be between −0.7 and −1.

The Statistical Significance

In any study involving correlation, an evaluator would want to know what the probability was that the correlation

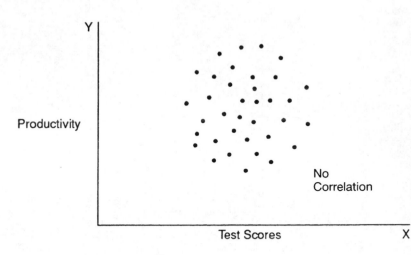

Fig. 8.7

could have happened by chance. If the correlation occured by chance, there would not be a real relationship between training and any improvement in performance.

Statisticians have calculated the minimum correlation values needed for given probabilities and sample sizes. By referencing the correlation coefficient obtained in a training evaluation study, for instance, with the values provided in a statistical table, one can obtain the statistical significance. For example, we may find that a correlation of .34 between a training test and units of productivity was significant at the .05 level. This means that there were less than five chances in 100 of obtaining that correlation of .34 by chance. The minimum acceptable level for inferring that a relationship exists is .05 or 5%. Significance levels are generally quoted at the .05 level and .01 level. The .01 level would mean that there was less than 1 chance in a hundred of obtaining the correlation value by accident.

Calculating the necessary sample size needed for a particular correlation coefficient value

The larger the sample size, the smaller the correlation has to be significant at a particular level. The smaller the sample size, the larger the correlation coefficient needs to be at a particular level. A high correlation coefficient may have occured simply because the sample size was very small. In addition, a statistically significant correlation may not be very high if the sample size is very high and, therefore, not be very useful.

The table on the following page illustrates the sample size necessary to produce a particular correlation coefficient at a particular significance level. As an illustration of this concept, with a large sample size, say 100, the correlation coefficient would need to be 0.164 to be significant at the .05 level. With only a sample size of 5, however, one would need a stronger correlation coefficient at the .05 level, say 0.98.

Cause versus Relationship

Though it might be tempting to definitely say that training caused an increase in productivity or a decrease in absentee rates, correlations do not demonstrate cause. The best one can do is to point out that a relationship between the two variables exists.

Hypothesis Testing

In some cases, you may want to test out a hypothesis about a training programme. For example, you may want to find

Pearson Product Moment Correlation Coefficient
Significance levels, (1 tailed test.)

Sample Size	5%	2%	1%
2	0.988	0.997	0.999
3	0.900	0.950	0.980
4	0.805	0.818	0.934
5	0.729	0.811	0.882
10	0.521	0.602	0.685
15	0.426	0.497	0.574
20	0.369	0.433	0.503
25	0.330	0.388	0.453
30	0.330	0.355	0.416
35	0.275	0.325	0.381
40	0.257	0.304	0.358
45	0.243	0.288	0.338
50	0.231	0.273	0.322
60	0.211	0.250	0.295
70	0.195	0.232	0.274
80	0.183	0.217	0.256
90	0.173	0.205	0.242
100	0.164	0.195	0.230

out if clerical workers' performance improved as a result of training on word processing skills. The premise is either rejected or not rejected as a result of a statistical analysis. There are several formulas used in testing hypotheses; the formula used depends on the type of data being compared.

A test that would apply in evaluation of training is called a "one-tailed test".

Errors in Rejecting or not Rejecting the Hypothesis

No matter which choice is made about the hypothesis, that choice has the possibility of being inaccurate. If the hypothesis is true and it is rejected, the error is called a Type I error. If the hypothesis is false and it is not rejected, the error is called a Type II error. One can determine the probability of making an error by consulting a statistical table for what is called the "significance level". For example, a .05 significance level means that there is a 5% chance that a Type I error has been made. The lower the significance level, the more possibility of error; the higher the significance level (.10 or .20 for example) the higher the possibility of error. The calculations for hypothesis testing are beyond the scope of this book. A statistician, or someone with experience in hypothesis testing, should be consulted if hypothesis testing is undertaken.

Mixing Evaluation Techniques: Triangulating the Data

If you use only one evaluation technique, especially if it captures only one perspective, your results may not tell the whole story. Consider this scenario. Suppose that you've completed an evaluation study of a communications training course for middle managers. You've used pre- and post-self-reporting questionnaires to gauge whether or not the middle managers have improved their communication skills. Unfortunately, the opinions of managers about their own skills may be suspect. What about the perspective of their immediate bosses? Or observations from an unbiased evaluator of their skills both before and after the training? Using more than one source of data in the evaluation design is called triangulating the data. Triangulation contributes to verification and validation of your findings because you are able to check out the consistency of different data.

The evaluation can be triangulated in three different ways:

■ Different research methods can be used (for example, qualitative and quantitative methods)
■ Different techniques can be used within a research methodology (for example, within qualitative methods both observation and interviews could be done).
■ Multiple evaluators can be used, (for example, bosses, peers, and a training specialist might observe the trainees.)

It is important to think about triangulating the data in the design phase of the evaluation process. Ask yourself these key guestions:

■ Whose perspectives are important in measuring whether or not the programme was successful?
■ Who are the stakeholders (who will be affected by the training?)
■ Is gathering both qualitative and quantitative data desirable?
■ What could easily be collected, in addition to what I have planned, that would help verify my findings?
■ Would collecting data at different points in time be beneficial?

Summary

■ *Statistics will help you summarise data, show relationships between two variables, and make inferences from a group of trainees to a larger population.*

■ *Computers can help you by eliminating hand calculation of statistical formulas and by graphically displaying information.*

■ *Use triangulation methods to ensure that your evaluation considers several points of view and several methodologies.*

Calculating the Costs Versus the Benefits of Training

An important part of an evaluation report, in addition to your research findings, will be the overall costs of the training versus the benefits derived from it. In a recent survey conducted by IRS, 68% of over 100 organisations calculate the cost of their training.[†] There are several ways of calculating costs versus benefits. What to include in the calculations, in part, will depend on what is traditionally acceptable in your organisation. One model is described below.

[†] Employment Development Bulletin, *Training Evaluation: An IRS Survey*, (May, 1992) p. 2

Determining Costs

Several items may be included in calculating costs. The most common ones are discussed here.

Personnel Costs:

Determine all the steps involved in putting the training together and the individuals involved in contributing to those steps. These might be design, writing, editing, video production, consulting fees etc. Determine the amount of time spent at each step of the process. Multiply the hourly or daily salary rate of each contributor × the amount of time each spent on the project. For example, perhaps a writer's wages are £40 per hour. She spent 200 hours on the project. The personnel costs for the writer are 200 × £40 or £8,000.

Training Materials:

Be sure to include everything that contributed to the delivery of the training. Materials might include audio-visual aids such as filmstrips, movies, slides, acetates, notebooks for participants, audio-cassettes, and models. All production costs should be calculated as material costs. Production costs might include photocopying, typesetting materials, printing, manuals, leader's guides, word processing costs, and course certificates.

Delivery Costs:

Delivery costs usually include the salaries of instructors and trainees, travel expenses such as mileage, airfares, taxis, meals, and hotels. Conference and syndicate room fees are included here as well as anything related to delivery of the course such as pencils, pens, nametags, and flipcharts.

To calculate the total costs add up the delivery costs, personnel costs, and material costs.

Determining Benefits

Calculating benefits is more difficult than determining costs simply because many benefits are intangible. Improved attitudes, better staff morale and increased knowledge are difficult to quantifiy in terms of pounds. Although difficult, there are ways to calculate these intangible benefits. Benefits may include any of the following:

Materials:

Materials costs can be reduced by improving inventory procedures or by improving stocking methods. A company might improve its bottom-line by ridding itself of an inefficient inventory system. Sales might have been lost because inventory was not in stock when it was needed.

Time:

Time savings are commonly figured as part of the benefits of training. Improved understanding of how to run equipment or better working relationships might improve productive time. To calculate time savings determine whose time was saved and their hourly wage. For example, assume managers say they are more efficient as a result of a time management training course. They report that they are getting an additional hour's worth of work done that before the training they frittered away. To calculate the savings to the company, multiply the average hourly rate for managers × the number of managers in the training course.

Equipment:

Calculating cost savings from elimination or reduction of downtime is most useful in manufacturing environments. First, determine the value of the equipment. Divide the costs of the equipment by the number of hours it will be used. To determine improved productivity, simply multiply the hours of increased usage by the equipment value.

Calculating the costs of downtime is similar to calculating improved productivity. If a machine is unusable for two days, the cost of downtime is the daily usage rate for the machine × 2 (let's say 10 hours × 2 or 20 hours) multiplied by the equipment value (let's say £20 per hour) or £400.

Personnel Turnover and Improved Retention:

Replacing staff is an expensive process. New staff have to be recruited and trained. The costs of advertising positions, the lost time in production when positions are left empty, and the cost of training can be substantial. You might want to examine retention rates of the group you are training both pre- and post-training. For example, you might find that retention rates improved in supervisors after several courses in management techniques. Perhaps retention rates improved by 20% among the 100 supervisors. This represents 20 individuals who were saved. Assume the costs of recruiting and training new supervisors is £10,000. The savings to the company is 20 × 10,000 or £200,000.

Avoiding Other Personnel Problems:

You can put a pound value on the savings of avoiding

specific problems such as absenteeism, strikes, and litigation. For example, a retailing group conducted training programmes for store clerks on sexual harassment in the workplace. It calculated the potential savings on litigation or industrial tribunal costs from the avoidance of employee complaints. It is possible to determine the costs of absenteeism by calculating the average employee costs per day by the improved employee absentee rate. For example, let's assume that after the training employee absenteeism rates improved by 25% which represented a savings of 20 days. Assume the average daily rate of the employees concerned is £60. The savings to the company is 20 days × £60 pounds or £1200.

Weighing Up the Costs Versus the Benefits

Add up all the benefits of the training programme and compare them to the costs incurred. Even if your costs outweigh the benefits you may make a case for training as an investment.

Training as an Investment (Calculating the Payback Period)

Some organisations willingly accept the fact that training is an investment in people that takes time to show positive results. If you are unable to show an immediate savings from the result of a training programme, you may be able to demonstrate a return or a break even figure in over two or three or five years. To calculate the payback period, divide the total investment by the annual savings. For example, assume a programme has cost a total of £60,000 and each year the savings or benefits from the programme equal £20,000. The payback period on the initial investment of the training is 3 years: £60,000 divided by £20,000. This approach is powerful if individuals view training as critical to the strategic direction of the company. In determining whether or not this approach would be useful ask yourself these questions: Is the activity or skill I am training on vital to the smooth operation of the company? Can I tie the training activity to the future strategic direction of the company? Are all costs in the company evaluated on an annual basis? In other words, has this approach been used elsewhere in the company before?

The Utility Equation

The cost benefit on training can be calculated by a formula called the Utility Equation. This method of determining the benefits of training, developed by Schmidt, Hunter and Pearlman, is more complicated than other methods, but it is worth considering. The Utility Equation has also been used by psychologists, Cronbach and Glaser, to calculate the cost benefit of using tests in selection procedures. The formula looks at:

- the pound value of the training programme
- the length of time the training programme has had an effect on performance
- the number of people trained
- the difference in job performance between the average *trained* and the average *untrained* individuals in units of standard deviation

- the standard deviation of job performance of the untrained groups in pounds
- the cost per head of training

The formula is as follows:

£gain (utility) = T N dt SDy − N C

where:

T = the number of years a training programme has had an effect on performance

N = the number of employees trained

dt = the difference in job performance between the average trained and the average untrained in standard deviation units.

SDy = the standard deviation of job performance of the untrained group in pounds.

C = the cost per head of training

The validity of the programme in terms of the true difference (dt) between the average trained and the average untrained employees is the most difficult to calculate because it may be the most subjective. One way to determine it is to devise a standard performance rating scale for supervisors to rate their employees, both trained and untrained. Another somewhat subjective part of the formula is SDy, the standard deviation of job performance of the untrained group. This would need to be estimated by some expert opinion in the organisation, perhaps supervisors or managers.

Remember, in order to run the formula you need to calculate the standard deviation (the variability) of job performance. The formula for standard deviation is:

$$SD = \sqrt{\frac{\Sigma(X - \bar{X})^2}{N}}$$

where:

$\bar{X}$ = the mean

Σ = the sum of

X = the raw score (of performance)

N = the number of employees in the group

The Costs of Not Training

Some training programmes can effectingly demonstrate the potential costs associated if training were not done. For example, what would the costs be to an organisation that did not do safety training on potentially dangerous equipment? In this scenario, the training department could produce the costs associated with accidents: industrial tribunal costs, poor public relations, reduced employee morale and confidence. In another situation, the training department wanting to produce training on customer care could produce costs associated with becoming less competitive or losing market share. In many companies, service is the distinguishing factor that separate them from their competitors. Demonstrating what could happen if employees were not quality conscience and sensitive to customer needs may produce a strong enough case.

Choosing the Method of Justification

It is important to involve others in the decision about which method to employ. If you have set up an evaluation committee ask them for their input. Otherwise, consult with your accounting or finance department to see what they would suggest.

Summary

- *There are several ways to justify training in the organisation. A few common ways are:*
  - *cost benefit analysis*
  - *calculating the payback period*
  - *calculating the utility of training*
  - *calculating the costs of not training.*
- *In determining which method to use, consider how closely the training is linked to strategic initiatives (how important do individuals think the training is) and what would be acceptable in the organisation.*
- *Include other managers or an evaluation committee in helping you to determine which method to use.*

Putting Together an Evaluation Report

The purpose of an evaluation report is to explain the findings of the evaluation study to individuals who may not have been involved in it. Usually senior members of an organisation are interested in knowing what outcomes the training produced, especially if the training department is a cost centre rather than a profit centre. Department heads, who may have requested training for their staffs, will want to know what affect the training had on their employees. Producing an evaluation report is a good way of raising the profile of training in the organisation and, depending on the results of the evaluation, can help you sell the concept of additional training.

What to Include in an Evaluation Report

The evaluation report should include the following:

1. **Background About the Evaluation**
   Why was the evaluation study done? Who was evaluated? Who were the evaluators? When and where did the evaluation take place?

2. **Research Questions**
   What questions did the evaluation study attempt to answer?

3. **Methodologies Used**
   What research methods were used? Why were they chosen? Why were other methods rejected? What research design was used? What sample size of trainees was chosen? What timeframes were applied to the evaluation? Why were these timeframes chosen?

4. **Findings**
   Based on interviews, observations, surveys or other research methods, what was discovered? What answers are there to the original evaluation questions? What patterns or themes emerged from the qualitative data? This section of the report might be organised according to each major research question.

5. **Credibility of the Findings**
   If statistical significance tests were applied to any of the data they should be mentioned here. How significant are the findings? Besides the training, what else might have caused changes in the trainees? What other events, programmes or factors in the organisation might have influenced the evaluation study?

6. Conclusions and Recommendations

Summarise basic findings here. Include a cost versus benefit analysis of the training to demonstrate whether or not the training was "worth it". Depending on the data, recommendations might be any one or more of the following:

- further investigation of the findings.
- maintaining the current programme as it stands.
- decreasing the number of participants in order to focus on a particular target population.
- increasing the number of participants in the programme.
- terminating the programme.
- changing the content of the programme.
- building on the current programme to meet new demands. This might mean creation of additional training courses.

7. Appendix

An appendix should contain those documents that individuals may want to refer to for further understanding of your methods or the findings. You may want to include selected transcripts from interviews, interview formats, and survey or questionnaire formats.

Gaining Your Reader's Attention

Readers will be most interested in your findings. Try to balance the amount of background information and description with your findings and recommendations. You will not be able to include everything. When using qualitative data, pick the quotations that represent the feelings of the participants – do not try to include all of them. The report should flow easily and present a picture of the experience of the training from the trainee's perspective. If your readers are particularly busy and your organisation is used to reports that are short and succinct, consider moving the Research Questions, Findings, and Recommendation sections of the report to the front, followed by background information such as background on the evaluation, methodologies used.

Helping Your Reader Weigh-Up the Evidence

Not all of the data you collect will be equally significant. Guide the reader by explaining which pieces of data are more reliable. For example, you may find that your observation data is stronger than your interview data because of the inherent bias that the participants have about reporting, via the interview format, on their own progress. If you have used several data collection methods (for example, surveys, observations, and interviews) and they all suggest similar things, point this out to the reader. The strength of your findings is increased by the fact that you have triangulated them (see page 95). In addition to explaining when you have used multiple data collection methods, explain when you have used multiple evaluators. If you have gained information from bosses, peers, and trainees, for example, which all suggests the same findings, the strength of your findings increases.

Giving an Oral Presentation

If you have the opportunity to make a presentation on the evaluation study, take advantage of it. The impact of an oral presentation will almost always be better than distributing a written report. When giving an evaluation presentation follow these guidelines:

- Make slides or overheads of the key points you want to make. You might consider taking some slides of the trainees at various stages of the training or during various stages of the evaluation (during interviews or observations). These visuals are inexpensive and can help the audience visualise the evaluation process.
- If you have a tight timeframe within which to present the evaluation study, be sure to start with the Research Questions, Findings and Recommendations. The last thing you want to have happen is to get through only half of your presentation without having had a chance to describe the finding or make your recommendations.
- Consider having others assist in the presentation. You may want to bring in another evaluator to help explain the methodologies used or a trainee to describe the overall impact of the programme. If you do use other presenters, keep their roles simple. Practice the presentation before presenting it 'live'. Provide other presenters with visuals such as slides or overheads. It is important that each presenter keeps to his or her allotted time.
- Use the written evaluation report as back-up information, passing it out at the end of your presentation. If you hand it out at the beginning of your presentation, you risk having the analyticals in your audience paging through the document rather than listening to you.
- Make a list of the possible questions that your audience might ask. Formulate a response to each question.
- When you practice the presentation, do so in front of someone unfamiliar with the content of the evaluation. Ask

the individual to ask questions or to play the devil's advocate to your findings or recommendations.

Summary

- *Write up an evaluation report to solidify your findings.*
- *Include the following in an evaluation report: background about the evaluation, research questions, methodologies used, findings, conclusions and recommendations.*
- *Try to find a forum to formally present your findings; an oral presentation can be a very effective way of describing your research findings and of gaining support for future training efforts.*

List of Useful Addresses

For information on how to evaluate quality assurance programmes or training related to Total Quality Management:

> The Institute of Quality Assurance
> 8–10 Grovenor Gardens
> London
> SW1W 0DQ

> British Standards Institution
> Linford Wood
> Milton Keynes MK 14 6LE

For information about evaluation and the Investors In People Award:

> Contact your local Training and Enterprise Council (TEC).

For information about using computers in evaluation:
SPSS UK Ltd
SPSS House
5 London Street
Chertsey
Surrey, KT16 8AP

For information about the National Training Award:
National Training Awards Office
Room W823
Moorfoot,
Sheffield S1 4PQ

Bibliography

American Society For Training And Development. (1990).
How To Conduct A Cost-Benefit Analysis (Info-line Rep. No.
007). Alexandria, VA.: Author.

Anderson, S.B. & Ball, S. (1978). *The Professional Practice Of
Programme Evaluation*. London: Jossey-Bass.

National Training Awards (1991) (2/12/91) *The Times*

National Training Award Office (1993). National Training
Awards Winners: Synopses & Report – Success Stories of
the 1992 Winners. Sheffield.

Newby, T. (1992). *Training Evaluation Handbook*. Aldershot,
U.K.: Gower.

Patton, M.Q. (1986) *Qualitative Evaluation Methods* (7th ed.).
London: Sage.

Phillips, J. (1991). *Handbook of Evaluation and Measurement
Methods* (2nd ed.). London: Gulf.

Roberts, J. (January, 1989). Training is the key. *Employment
Gazette*, 7–13.

Schmidt, F.L., Hunter, J.E. and Pearlman, K. *(1982) Assessing the Economic Impact of Personnel Programs on Workforce Productivity* Personnel Psychology vol. 35 pp. 333–347 (1982).

Training Evaluation: An IRS Survey. (May, 1992). *Employment Development Bulletin,* 2–12.

Warr, P., Bird, M. & Rackman, N. (1979). *Evaluation of Management Training* (6th ed.). Farnborough, England: Gower.

Weikowitz, J., Ewen, R. & Cohen, (1982). *Introductory Statistics for the Behavioral Sciences* (3rd ed.). London: Harcourt Brace Jovanovich.

Yin, R. (1989). *Case Study Research: Design and Methods* (rev. ed.). London: Sage.